SPIRIT OF

CAMBRIDGE

GRAHAM UNEY

PiXZ

First published in Great Britain in 2009
Reprinted 2014

British Library Cataloguing-in-Publication Data
A CIP record for this title is available from the British Library

ISBN 978 1 906887 08 7

PiXZ Books
Halsgrove House, Ryelands Business Park,
Bagley Road, Wellington, Somerset TA21 9PZ
Tel: 01823 653777
Fax: 01823 216796
email: sales@halsgrove.com

An imprint of Halstar Ltd, part of the Halsgrove group of companies
Information on all Halsgrove titles is available at: www.halsgrove.com

Printed and bound in China by Toppan Leefung

Introduction

The magnificent buildings, both historic and modern, of the City of Cambridge have always been a splendid centrepiece to the county of Cambridgeshire. Tourists and students from around the world now throng the twisting streets, mixing with the locals who happily go about their daily business, many of them oblivious to the traditional but inevitable split between 'town and gown'.

That said, Cambridge is much more than one of the prime university cities of the world. The town was an important settlement hundreds of years before the first scholars arrived here. The town grew at the point where the River Cam could most easily be crossed by those travelling from the forests of the south and east into the fens of the north, or vice versa.

When the Romans occupied Cambridge, they moved into a township that had already been well established since the Iron Age. A Belgic tribe had recognised the importance of this fording place and had settled on both banks of the river.

Eventually, as they did throughout Britain, the Romans left Cambridge, being called back to Rome to deal with the invading Visigoths who had been displaced from Romania by the marauding Huns.

The Saxons moved in to Cambridge, followed by the Normans, and their architecture can still be seen in a few places today.

The trade routes that brought travellers to the crossing place over the Cam, as well as the importance of the river itself for moving goods back and forth, helped to establish Cambridge as the most advanced centre in East Anglia, and when the Oxford riots broke out in 1209, a group of students wasted no time in moving east to Cambridge. The first new college was Peterhouse, founded by the Bishop of Ely in 1284. Others soon followed, adding their own architectural merit to the mediaeval buildings of the city.

This book takes you on a tour of the central part of the City of Cambridge through a collection of vividly colourful images. *Spirit of Cambridge* is a book about this city, its streets and alleyways, its colleges and public offices, its local people and its tourists, and the wide variety of open spaces and commons that the city folk enjoy today. It's also a book about the River Cam, the flats of which were so instrumental in the establishment of this great city in the first place.

I now live in Cambridgeshire, just outside the city, after a lifetime of exploring Britain. I hope my passion for this remarkable county capital shines through in the pages of this book.

Graham Uney

For most people heading into the city via Trumpington Street, the imposing entrance to the Fitzwilliam Museum is the one of the first important buildings they see. The museum houses a number of important world-class collections of works of art and antiquities, and has free entry.

Just across the road from the Fitzwilliam Museum you'll see the splendid façade of the Judge Institute, now the Judge Business School.

Peterhouse College was the first to be established in Cambridge. It was founded in 1284 by Hugo de Balsham, the Bishop of Ely. It is also the smallest of Cambridge's colleges, with 250 undergraduates, 90 graduate students, and 45 fellows.

Pembroke College lies a little way along Trumpington Street from Peterhouse, and on the other side of the road. Its grounds and courts are a real haven after the bustle of the outside world.

The doorway to the font of all knowledge! The Porter's Lodge at Peterhouse College.

Pembroke College was founded in 1347 by Marie de St Pol, the Countess of Pembroke, and as such is the third oldest of Cambridge's colleges. Other notable features of the college include the first chapel to be designed by Sir Christopher Wren, and this stunning sculpture of William Pitt the Younger, a fellow of the college who went on to become the youngest British Prime Minister at the age of 24, in 1783.

Corpus Christi College is easy to miss, but pass through the gatehouse doors and you are confronted by the splendid New Court. The College of Corpus Christi and the Blessed Virgin Mary, to give it its full title, was founded in 1352.

The doorway into the Old Court at Corpus Christi.

Head through the Old Court in Corpus Christi College and you'll find yourself backing on to Bene't Street Church, Cambridge's oldest surviving building. The tower dates from around 1025. These gravestones lean up against the college wall.

Right:
On Friday 19th September 2008, Professor Stephen Hawkin unveiled the new Corpus Clock. Dubbed 'The Strangest Clock in the World', its inventor, Dr John Taylor, said he, "wanted to make timekeeping interesting". It is known as a 'chronophage' which means 'time-eater', and it stands on the corner of Bene't Street.

Left:
The fine old buildings and sundial in Old Court, Corpus Christi College.

Punting is one of the greatest pastimes in Cambridge.

Left:
One of the classic views of the River Cam, the Mathematical Bridge spanning the river behind Queens' College. The bridge was built in 1749 by James Essex the Younger, to the design of William Etheridge. It has subsequently been rebuilt to the same design twice.

THE ANCHOR
SILVER STREET

Left:

Even in the rain, punting is big business on the River Cam. Here, outside The Anchor on Silver Street, a boat-load of tourists heads back in, umbrellas at the ready.

Right:

Cycling is the main way of getting around Cambridge, and there are countless bike shops scattered throughout the city. Look for this one tucked away in Laundress Lane.

King's College was founded in 1441, and was one of the first all-male colleges to admit women. It is proud of its reputation for welcoming students from both state and public schools.

The impressive frontage of King's College.

Above, left: King Henry VI laid the foundation stones for King's College, fully intending the buildings to be a magnificent display of the power of the monarchy. He went to great lengths to ensure that King's College Chapel would be unrivalled throughout the country.

Above, right: The Gatehouse at King's College leads into the Front Court. To the left stands Wilkins' Building, while the Gibbs' Building lies at the back of the court.

Punting on the Cam at King's College Bridge.

Peter Randall-Page was commissioned by Grosvenor to work on a sculpture for their Fisher's Square frontage in Cambridge. He came up with 'Between the Lines', a huge carved block of granite, which was unveiled in 2007.

CAFFÈ NERO

The Tower Clock, Great St Mary's Church.

Left:
Looking along King's Parade from King's College Gatehouse. The towers of Great St Mary's Church, and Gonville and Caius College stand at the end of the parade.

Great St Mary's Church dominates the western side of Market Hill.

Tucked in behind Great St Mary's Church is Market Hill.

Right:
Colourful stalls in Market Hill.

Mad clusters of chimneypots from Great St Mary's Church tower.

From the top of the tower in Great St Mary's Church, you get superb views of little-known parts of the city.

The Senate House Hill Old Schools date from the 1720s, and were constructed of Portland stone by architect James Gibbs. To the left stands King's College Chapel, while Senate House is to the right. At the centre of the lawn in the foreground is the Warwick Vase, erected in 1830.

Left:
Senate House is perhaps the best known University building in Cambridge, as distinct from college buildings. It is used today for graduation ceremonies.

Right:
Fine Portland stone columns guard the entrance to Senate House.

The Bell Tower at Gonville and Caius College. The college was founded by Edmund Gonville in 1348, but was refounded and expanded in 1557 by former student and Fellow, Dr John Caius. Dr Caius Latinised his name from the original spelling 'Keys' after living in Italy, and the college name is still pronounced 'Keys' to this day.

The view from Great St Mary's Church to Gonville and Caius College, and along Trinity Street towards Trinity College and St John's College in the distance.

Left:
Tucked away behind the colleges are 'The Backs'. Here, at Clare College, punting along the River Cam is a pleasant way to spend a sunny afternoon.

Right:
The gateway on Trinity Lane, leading into Clare College.

Clare College at dusk, from The Backs.

In spring thousands of daffodils line the paths along The Backs.

Right:
A punt waiting for the off, on the River Cam

Far right:
Punting at Trinity College Bridge, and the start of The Avenue, the line of trees that leads westwards towards the Fellows' Garden.

Trinity Hall's The Jerwood Library. This fine modern building, overhanging the Cam, was completed in September 1998, and was officially opened in May 1999. It stands over Garret Hostel Lane Bridge.

Rooftops of Clare College and Trinity Hall.

A fine view from Great St Mary's Church tower of Trinity College and St John's College.

Wander along Trinity Street and you'll soon find your gaze dominated by the tower of St John's College Chapel.

Trinity Street is one of Cambridge's busiest. It pulses with shoppers, while cyclists have to be on their guard to avoid running into pedestrians.

Look for the countless little statues and gargoyles on the old college buildings as you walk down Trinity Street.

Green Street is a fine old cobbled street leading between Trinity Street and Sidney Street.

Off to the east from Trinity Street there are a couple of great little shopping streets. This is Rose Crescent at dusk.

Right:
On the opposite side of Trinity Street is this superb view of the back of Trinity College. Trinity Lane leads down to the river at Garret Hostel Lane.

Opposite:
Trinity College was founded by Henry VIII in 1546, combining the old King's Hall and Michaelhouse. This is the Great Gate, built in the sixteenth century.

EDVARDVS P. WALLIE
VE BLACK PRINCE
EDVARDVS TERTIVS FVNDATOR
AVLE REGIS. MCCCXXXVII.
DE HATFELD
DE MORTVVS INFANS
W JOHN OF GAVNT.

Trinity College's Great Gate, from the Great Court.

In Trinity College's Great Court, The Fountain dominates.

Left:
The King Edward's Gate Clock at Trinity College. This is one of the oldest buildings within the college, and once formed the grand entrance to King's Hall, which was dissolved in 1546 to found the new college.

Right:
Nevile's Court and the Wren Library in Trinity College. Nevile's Court was built by Thomas Nevile in 1605, and comprised only three sides. The fourth, at the far end of the lawn, is the Wren Library. This was originally just a wall, but was replaced by the library in 1695. The local master mason, used rock from a Rutland quarry, and built the library to a design by Sir Christopher Wren.

St John's College was founded in 1511 by Lady Margaret Beaufort, mother of King Henry VII. It is the second largest of Cambridge's colleges.

The Third Court at St John's College.

Fine panelling on the ceiling of the Chapel entrance in Chapel Court, St John's College.

The Bridge of Sighs, St John's College. It was built when New Court was completed in 1831 to connect the New Court with the Third Court.

Left:
New Court is a fine example of nineteenth century architecture. It was completed in 1831 to the design of Thomas Rickman and Henry Hutchinson, and was the first major building to be placed by any college to the west of the River Cam.

Right:
The entrance to New Court, St John's College.

The style of New Court at St John's College is a romanticised version of a mediaeval building. This cloister forms the south side of the court.

A window through the cloister into New Court, St John's College.

Only four round churches survive in England, and the one in Cambridge on Bridge Street is a fine example. It was built around 1130 and started life as a wayfarer's chapel. It soon became the parish church of the Hospital of St John, which later became St John's College.

Inside the Round Church there is a fine exhibition about the history of the church, and of Christianity in Cambridgeshire.

Inside the Round Church.

Walking along Bridge Street, it's easy to forget that above the modern frontage of shops there are some superb ancient buildings.

Punting on the Cam at Magdalene Bridge.

Modern apartments overlook Magdalene College with the flats of the River Cam flowing between. This is one of the most popular parts of the river for punting.

In spring cherry blossom sprays over the river at Magdalene College.

Walk northwards from Magdalene Bridge and you'll find the crossroads where Magdalene Street meets Northampton Street, Castle Street, and Chesterton Lane. Here, on a corner, lies the Folk Museum, a great place to discover the social history of Cambridge. The museum is housed in the former White Horse Inn. Behind the museum is Kettle's Yard, a unique house containing the distinctive art collections of Jim Ede. Jim Ede was a former curator of the Tate Gallery, London.

The crossroads at the meeting of Magdalene Street, Northampton Street, Castle Street, and Chesterton Lane.

Sidney Sussex College lies to the south from Bridge Street. Bridge Street becomes Sidney Street and the college lies to the left, almost hidden behind its Gatehouse which is easy to miss. Sidney Sussex College is named after its foundress, Frances Sidney, Countess of Sussex. It was founded in 1596, and Oliver Cromwell was among its first students (although he never graduated).

Christ's College was founded in 1437 by William Byngham, a London parish priest. Originally, the college was housed in what was known as God's House, although it was forced to move premises as the site was needed for King Henry VI's new project (King's College). It moved to its present site in 1448 and in 1505, with a new charter from the King, was founded as Christ's College.

Christ's College is famous for a number of eminent scholars over the years, including John Milton, Charles Darwin, Lord Todd (the Nobel prize-winning chemist), and James Meade (Nobel laureate in economics).